Original title:
Frozen Lakes, Quiet Dreams

Copyright © 2024 Creative Arts Management OÜ
All rights reserved.

Author: Nathaniel Blackwood
ISBN HARDBACK: 978-9916-94-604-6
ISBN PAPERBACK: 978-9916-94-605-3

Stillness Wrapped in White

Snowflakes dance on the chilly breeze,
While squirrels slide with sneaky ease.
Ice-skates giggle like little mice,
As penguins strut—oh, aren't they nice?

A snowman waves with a crooked grin,
His carrot nose all crooked and thin.
The hat's too big and the scarf's askew,
In this white wonderland, how can we stew?

Dreams Adrift on Ice

A polar bear wearing shades so bright,
Sips hot cocoa by the pale moonlight.
Frogs in jackets jump on the run,
Trying to catch some winter sun.

Snowmen gossip about weather woes,
As ice fishers brag of all they knows.
A sleigh bell rings—come join the fun,
In this winter scene where all's undone!

Frost-kissed Reveries

Icicles sparkle like tiny lights,
While owls hoot in cozy nights.
Marshmallow clouds drift in the air,
As rabbits race without a care.

Chattering teeth from a snowball fight,
Whispers of snowflakes taking flight.
A snowshoe hare with a floppy ear,
Dances around—oh, what a cheer!

Silence in the Subzero Glow

A chilly breeze whirls round and round,
As friends play tag without a sound.
Penguins wearing scarves try to fly,
While frosty stars wink from the sky.

Fluffy jackets piled high with cheer,
Skating ducks slide by without fear.
Snowflakes fall in a comic spree,
In this quiet chill, let's dance with glee!

Stillness in the Moonlight

In the night, a bird fell flat,
Trying to land on a lazy cat.
Ice cream cones, they slipped away,
While giggling penguins came to play.

Socks might be in a fist fight,
Who knew they'd be so full of spite?
The moonlight's glow made them dance,
Spreading joy, not a single chance!

Crystal Reflections of Night

A raccoon in a tuxedo pranced,
In the shimmer, it bravely danced.
With a tophat, it tried to twirl,
But ended up in a dizzy whirl.

Muffins rolled across the ice,
The ducks all laughed, "Oh, that's nice!"
A snowman tried to take a leap,
In the cold, he made a heap!

Echoes of a Silent Slumber

Here lies a snail with a blanket on,
Dreaming of races from dusk till dawn.
A sleepy owl with a coffee cup,
Says, "Hey, guys, let's wake up!"

The stars are laughing at the show,
As giraffes practice ballet, oh so slow.
An igloo's got a disco ball,
Penguins dancing, that's the call!

Chilled Breezes over Glassy Waters

A fish in boots played tag with a frog,
While a bear attempted a doggy log.
The ice was slick, and laughter rose,
As a walrus posed in pinky clothes.

The breeze asked, "Why's the cat so sad?"
"Because my pants, they feel so bad!"
But in the chill, fun's always near,
With snowman jokes that bring good cheer!

Air Heavy with Dreams

The air's thick, like a gooey pie,
With whispers of secrets that often lie.
A duck wearing socks strolls past the scene,
While squirrels debate on the merits of beans.

Laughter echoes on the still, cold night,
As penguins juggle and put up a fight.
The moon winks slyly, a cheeky jest,
In the land where the fun never seems to rest.

Moonlit Secrets on the Ice

Beneath the glow of a cheeky moon,
A turtle dances to a silly tune.
The ice sings softly, 'Come join the spree!'
As snowflakes giggle, 'We're wild and free!'

A snowman spills frost, laughs with delight,
While rabbits do plies in the pale moonlight.
Jokes and puns slide on the ice like a kite,
In this quaint world that's purely a sight.

Slumbering Waters

Bubbles of giggles rise up from the deep,
As fish play poker and roll in a heap.
A bear, on a raft, is napping away,
While frogs claim they're stars in an offbeat play.

The otters are masters of slapstick flair,
Riding the current without a care.
Alligators smile at their goofy friends,
In the land where silliness never ends.

Stars Twinkling Through the Chill

Stars are chuckling, a cosmic tease,
While a fox tells tales to the chilly breeze.
The shadows dance, with a jig and a hop,
As the world gets ready for jokes that won't stop.

A moose wears a scarf, oh what a sight!
Wobbling through paths in the soft, pale light.
With laughter like snowflakes that glitter and shine,
Dreams take a bow, say 'It's all just divine!'

Crystal Shadows

In the park, the ice is slick,
Skaters glide, it's quite the trick.
Falling down, a comedic show,
"Watch me dance!"—who knew they'd go?

Silly hats and scarves galore,
Snowmen join the laughing score.
Glistening crystals catch the light,
But who knew ice could spark such fright?

The Calm Before Thaw

The sun is shy, but that's okay,
It's warming up for a new play.
Snowballs fly with giggles loud,
"Don't hit me!" shouts the brave and proud.

Chirping birds make quite a fuss,
Sipping tea on a bumpy bus.
Nature's breath, a frosty tease,
And winter laughs with playful ease.

Secrets of the Winter Depths

Underneath the glistening ice,
Fish are thinking, "Is this nice?"
They giggle at the clumsy skate,
"Just watch your toes, or seal your fate!"

The secrets held in chilly depths,
Are whispered by the frozen steps.
"Do a jump!" a beaver shouts,
While ice-cream cones without a doubt.

Echoes in the Chill

Echoes bounce off frosty walls,
Laughter echoes, someone falls.
In the distance, a snowball's flight,
A racing sledder with pure delight.

"Who left that mound?" The questions grow,
"Is that a hat or just some snow?"
With faces red and cheeks aglow,
Winter's humor steals the show.

The Stillness Between Breaths

In winter's clutch, all is still,
A penguin slips, what a thrill!
With ice so slick, it took a dive,
Now the laughter, oh how it thrives!

A squirrel skates, grab the hot cocoa,
He's got moves like a pro, oh no!
But instead of grace, he loses his tail,
And ends up in a snowy veil!

Nurtured by the Winter's Breath

The air is crisp, a frosty bite,
Snowflakes dance, what a sight!
But then a snowman starts to sneeze,
And down he goes with utmost ease!

Chattering teeth, what a fine show,
From a penguin wearing a bright yellow bow.
His waddles quick, his flair unmatched,
While snowballs fly, his dreams dispatched!

Veil of Snow and Silence

Wrapped in white, the world sleeps tight,
But a bunny hops, oh what a sight!
He leaps and bounds, trips on his ears,
Sending giggles and cheerful cheers!

A fox in a scarf, looking quite dapper,
Decides to tango, but ends up in a napper.
With frosty breath, he snores aloud,
The snowflakes gather, they form a crowd!

Shimmers of Hope in Frigid Waters

A fish swims by, with a wink so sly,
Under ice sheets, they giggle and sigh.
He tries to juggle, but slips a bit,
Creating splashes, perfect for a skit!

While skaters glide, they twirl and spin,
One takes a plunge with a goofy grin.
Laughter echoes, amid icy gleams,
In this magic place, we chase our dreams!

A Pathway of Silent Thoughts

Upon the ice, I skate with flair,
My boots are squeaking, what a pair!
I glide and slip, oh what a sound,
Spinning like a dizzy clown.

The trees are quiet, not a peep,
While I fall down, a snowy heap!
I laugh aloud, it echoes bright,
In this chilly realm of pure delight.

Respite Beneath the Frost

In winter's grip, we find a nook,
With cocoa warm, we cozy up the book.
The marshmallows dance, a sugary sight,
While outside, snowmen try to take flight!

Their carrot noses, oh what a shame,
One blew away, like it's playing a game.
With laughter, we poke, and tease away,
Until all the snowmen decide to play.

Night's Tranquil Feet

The moon's a disco, casting beams,
While I trip over my own silly dreams.
Stars are giggling, twinkling bright,
As I dance with shadows, what a sight!

Footprints in snow, a wobbly trace,
I whirl and twirl, losing face.
Nature chuckles, its secrets keep,
As I leap and tumble, peaceful sleep.

The Secret Life of Snow

Whispers of snowflakes flutter by,
They giggle softly, oh my oh my!
As they land on noses, they start a fight,
With laughter and joy, they gleefully alight.

Each flake a dream, a story to tell,
Of snowball battles, they know so well.
They tiptoe gently, soft and light,
Turning the world into pure delight.

Embrace of the White Landscape

In winter's grip, the world turns white,
Sledding down hills, what a funny sight!
Snowmen wobble with carrot noses,
As laughter blooms like wild, bright roses.

Hot cocoa spills while snowflakes dance,
We slip and slide, in a clumsy prance.
With mittens lost and hats a-flop,
Chasing our dreams, we never stop.

Sheltered by the Cold

Bundled up tight, like a marshmallow treat,
We fly down the slopes, oh what a feat!
Icicles hang like shimmering teeth,
And penguin-shaped sleds bring gasps underneath.

Frosty breath paints the air with glee,
We invent some games, just you and me.
Snow angels flop, then get back up,
With no sense of grace, just giggles and cup!

Heartbeats Beneath the Ice

Beneath the surface, a fish winks awake,
While skaters twirl like a cake on a break.
With flailing limbs, they glide and they flop,
The ice gives way to a comical crop.

Whispers of splashes in quiet repose,
As chilly winds tease the tips of our toes.
We sketch our dreams with a frost-covered pen,
Creating stories again and again!

The Calm Before the Thaw

Beneath the stillness, the chuckles reside,
As winter waves, we now must abide.
With sun peeking out, a melting surprise,
Puddles are forming; oh how time flies!

With snowmen drooping, they slowly decay,
We laugh as they wink, in a comical way.
A slushy adventure awaits on the street,
With flip-flop splashes, what a silly treat!

Dreams Adrift in the Still

In a winter field, a cow does moo,
It thought it was a penguin, too.
Ice skates on hooves, oh what a sight,
Waltzing with snowflakes, giddy with fright.

A squirrel steals from a fridge outside,
Mistook it for a winter ride.
With acorns packed like little treats,
He slides and slips on frozen sheets.

Moonbeams chuckle, stars take a peek,
The snowman sneezes, and he goes 'Eek!'
His carrot nose flops back on his face,
As he shuffles around, trying to keep pace.

The night is bright, the air is crisp,
But the penguin was just an icy wisp.
In the stillness, laughter roams free,
As dreams of snowball fights glide with glee.

Winter's Gentle Lullaby

A snowflake fell and took a bow,
Then slipped on ice, oh dear, oh wow!
A snowy owl laughs from a high tree,
'You dance like a chicken, not like me!'

All bundled up, a kid takes a plunge,
Straight into a drift, they all laugh and lunge.
Hot cocoa spills on mittens so bright,
It's a fashion statement, what a delight!

Frosty faces with noses red,
Giggles erupt, no one's misled.
They build a snowman, a lopsided boon,
With a twirling scarf and a silly tune.

As the moonlight glimmers on the frost,
Laughter echoes through the trees embossed.
In cozy moments, they play till past two,
For winter's lullaby is a joke for two.

A World Wrapped in Serenity

An overstuffed snowman rules the plaza,
With buttons that wobble, it's quite a drama.
The penguins online, a viral sensation,
They're skating on ice with no hesitation!

Underneath trees, branches droop low,
A raccoon in a hat, oh what a show!
He raids the snack stash, munching away,
While the world wraps him in fluffy display.

The snow is a canvas, they paint with their feet,
Making silly shapes that can't be beat.
With laughter like tinkling bells in the night,
Dreams dance in snow, weaving pure delight.

As the stars twinkle, the night yawns wide,
Wonders of winter, they cannot hide.
In silence, joy prints a warm souvenir,
A world wrapped in laughter, and neighbors near.

The Song of Snowflakes

The snowflakes waltz on a spectral breeze,
While birds in hats sing songs with ease.
With each gust and twirl, they trip and yell,
They're all rehearsing for a winter's spell!

A bunny hops, wearing mismatched socks,
He hops and trots, avoiding the blocks.
With snowball fights under a twinkling sky,
His epic fails make no one ask why.

The hot chocolate flows, a river of fun,
With marshmallows floating, they've already won.
A game of snow tag, they scuttle and dash,
'Catch me if you can!' and there's quite a splash.

As laughter drips from the frosty air,
The song of flakes lingers everywhere.
In this whimsical moment, joy takes flight,
In a snow-dusted world, everything feels right.

The Weight of Still Air

The chilly breeze won't say a thing,
It just floats past like a feathered king.
Penguins strut in a tuxedo style,
While I trip over my own frozen smile.

My toes are numb, but oh the sight!
A snowman's hat flies off in flight.
He waves goodbye with a carrot nose,
As I slip and slide, doing ballet toes!

Midnight Musings on Ice

Stars twinkle down on the frosty glaze,
Thoughts drift like ice skaters in a daze.
I ponder why penguins waddle with flair,
While I just wish to find a warm chair.

The moon plays tricks, it's a bright spotlight,
I dance with shadows, hoping for flight.
Falling flat on a smooth, glassy floor,
I'm the main act in the ice show's encore!

Grace of the Silent Mirror

The surface gleams like a polished shoe,
Reflecting me in an awkward view.
I wave to my twin, who's me in reverse,
He grins back with a smile - oh, what a curse!

I come to terms with my icy fate,
But in this mirror, I look first-rate!
Yet every slip is a chance to learn,
That laughter is warmth in this glacial turn.

Frosted Echoes of the Heart

Chirping crickets turn into ice-skating frogs,
As snowflakes twirl like lazy dialogue.
My heart echoes with laughter so bright,
While squirrels debate if snow's worth a bite.

Each shimmer and sparkle, a whisper of cheer,
Makes me wonder if spring will appear.
Till then I'll dance in these frosty cascades,
And giggle at all of the winter charades!

Twilight's Quiet Watch

A squirrel skates with style, oh so neat,
Chasing his lunch on skates, what a feat!
The trees all giggle, they sway in delight,
As snowflakes laugh softly, all through the night.

The moon casts a grin, it's a comic ballet,
With frosty breath, the night critters play.
A walrus slipped once, not quite under wraps,
And snowmen chuckled, avoiding the traps.

Under the Weight of Snow

Pigeons are waddling, strutting so proud,
Looking for snacks, beneath the white shroud.
Their feathers are puffy, their strut full of glee,
Each flurry is fashion, oh how stylish they be!

The snowballs are flying, a cheeky old game,
As kids throw their laughs, and giggles the same.
A penguin slips by, holding a snack,
Loudly declaring, 'I've got more in my pack!'

Glassy Horizons at Dawn

The sun peeks out, with a wink and a grin,
A duck quacks the news, let the fun times begin!
The ice shimmers bright, like a shiny new toy,
While beavers hold parties, oh what a joy!

Paddleboats hover, on mirrors so clear,
As frosty-faced foxes come in for a cheer.
With snow hats and canes, they dance on thin air,
While bunnies in tuxedos can't help but declare!

Murmurs of Crystal Dreams

The otters are gossiping, sliding with flair,
Making jokes about ice, as they splash everywhere.
The chilly wind chuckles, it swirls and it twirls,
While polar bears join in for some frosty swirls.

An icicle droops, and a chorus of laughs,
As penguins parade in their wobbly paths.
Joy fills the air, with a fun little twist,
Where winter's a party, nothing's amiss!

The Embrace of Icy Nights

When penguins slide in fancy shoes,
They twirl and spin, what silly views!
A dance of frost on a moonlit scene,
Who knew the ice could be so keen?

The snowflakes giggle as they fall,
They tickle noses, one and all.
The chilly winds play tag in glee,
Who knew cold could be so free?

Chairs made of ice and tables too,
Serving lemonade that's frozen blue.
The fish dreaming of a sunny day,
Just might swim in their own ballet!

So let's toast with flurries of snow,
To the silliness that winter can show!
In icy moments laughter shines,
A frosty world full of silly signs.

In the Hash of the Frost

A snowman's hat upon a cat,
Wobbly, fuzzy, imagine that!
With carrot nose and mitten hands,
He struts around like rock star bands!

The squirrels slip and slide with cheer,
Wearing scarves, they toast with beer.
Polar bears come for the show,
With fuzzy socks, they steal the dough!

A penguin wearing a tutu bright,
Attempts a leap, quite the sight!
He tumbles down with a graceful flip,
Winter circus, tightrope trip!

So gather 'round, be bold and brave,
Let's rave like it's our own ice wave!
With laughter echoing so wide,
The frost will never dampen pride!

Whispered Yesterdays

In a snow globe, memories spin,
Old snowmen grinning, wearing thin.
With topsy turvy, they share a toast,
To the warm sun that they miss the most!

Icicles dangle, making a fuss,
They chatter loudly without a bus.
Can you hear the jokes in the wind?
Even frosty spirits look quite grinned!

An owl in pajamas, reading aloud,
Riddles of snow that make him proud.
With a flick of his wing, he shouts a pun,
About how ice cream leads to fun!

As stars twinkle, glimmer, and twine,
Let's craft a skit with a frosty line!
For in glistening cold with hearty laughter,
A tale unfolds, but it's just the after!

Repose in a World of Ice

Under blankets of frost, we all snore,
With snowball fights that we can't ignore!
Hypnotized by winter's embrace,
Even the penguins find their place!

A moose in a beanie struts quite proud,
While rabbits hop in a cotton cloud.
They share their secrets, tales, and dreams,
In this chilly realm, nothing's as it seems!

The frost has tales of a dance-off grand,
Where snowmen and critters all take a stand.
With epic moves and a spin around,
The frostbit laughter is the only sound!

So pull your boots, let's play today,
In a world where snowflakes laugh and sway!
For even in ice, joy we'll find,
Crafting our happiness, cleverly designed!

Beneath the Glimmering Surface

A slick expanse, smooth as pie,
Where ducks slide past, oh my, oh my!
They quack with glee, but it's no jest,
Their waddle's a dance, at nature's fest.

Beneath the sheen, the fish just snooze,
In their cozy homes, they cannot lose.
With dreams of worms, they drift away,
While skaters dash, laughing all day.

A child on skates takes a daring trip,
Spinning around with a floppy flip.
He lands in snow and bursts with cheer,
The chill of winter brings laughter near.

So grab your folks, let's take a chance,
We'll twirl and shout, and even prance.
The surface gleams, a joker's crown,
In this frosty world, let's clown around!

A Tranquil Veil of Ice

The ground's a canvas, white and bright,
As snowflakes dance in soft moonlight.
A silent pause, where giggles burst,
In snowball fights, we quench our thirst.

A deer tiptoes with grace so grand,
Unaware of the laughter, close at hand.
While snowmen sport hats and a grin,
They guard the dreams that float within.

Sleds race past, flying like jets,
With parents chasing, placing bets.
Who'll crash first in a twinkling heap?
It's all in fun, so laughs run deep!

As twilight fades, we share a song,
About our wins and how things went wrong.
In this frosty realm, fun's the aim,
Where every moment's a snow-filled game!

The Art of Winter's Stillness

A canvas white, with shadows cast,
As snowflakes swirl in a breezy blast.
With mittens tight and noses red,
We map our dreams, where giggles spread.

The trees don cloaks of winter's art,
While critters scamper, playing their part.
A snowman grins with a carrot nose,
As laughter spills where the chilly wind blows.

Here squirrels flatter, and ice skates squeak,
With rhythms of winter we all will seek.
The beauty serene, yet laughter flies,
As we stumble along, much to our surprise.

So take a moment, breathe it in,
Amidst the snow, we find our kin.
In this charming stillness, joy will light,
Our jolly hearts in the frosty night!

Sleep of the Shimmering World

The world lies still, wrapped up tight,
Under the blanket of dazzling white.
A sleepy cat finds a sunny spot,
Dreaming of fish with a hearty plot.

The birds may freeze but still they sing,
About the joys that winter can bring.
Fluffy rabbits hop with such delight,
In this dreamland, everything feels right.

The icy pond hosts a party of frogs,
Who slip and slide like dancing logs.
With croaks and quirks that make us grin,
Under the stars with friends so kin.

As laughter echoes through the night,
With every giggle, the world feels bright.
In this slumber, all our fun's unfurled,
Chasing dreams in this shimmering world!

Icy Reflections

A penguin slipped and did a dance,
On shiny ice, he took a chance.
He twirled around, all in good fun,
While others watched and laughed, they run.

A polar bear with shades so bright,
Waddled near to join the fight.
He tried to skate, fell on his back,
And now he's planning his next attack.

A moose appeared, he had a goal,
To ice fish near a frozen hole.
But each cast met with slippery fate,
And made him grumble, "This is great!"

A snowman with a carrot nose,
Woke up one day, thought he could pose.
But every snap sent him a-shiver,
He smiled wide, "I'm just a giver!"

Whispers Beneath the Snow

Under blankets cold and white,
Squirrels chatter in delight.
They plan a heist for winter's treat,
Nuts and berries for their feast!

A rabbit hops with secret flair,
Dancing high in frosty air.
While all the bunnies cheer and say,
"Who knew it'd be a hop-tastic day?"

Each flake that falls is like a laugh,
From fluffy clouds, a chilly bath.
They twinkle down with little cheer,
While winter's jokes are crystal clear.

A wise old owl hoots with glee,
"In winter's game, take it easy!"
He snickers loud with feathery grace,
"Just don't forget, you've got no place!"

Still Waters in Winter's Embrace

A skater glides, the world a blur,
Face cheeks red, his hat a stir.
He does a spin, then hits the ground,
The laughter echoes all around.

A dog on ice, such joy to find,
Running fast but slipping behind.
He spins like a top, then takes a pause,
Wags his tail, gives winter applause.

Two friends slide in a race to win,
But trip on snow, and laugh with sin.
They roll and tumble, side by side,
In the winter's chill, they bide.

The silence breaks with giddy squeals,
As kids pretend to be the seals.
Chasing each other, full of mirth,
"Who knew this frost could bring such birth?"

Serenity on Crystalline Surfaces

An ice skater with a quirky style,
Performs a move, it takes a while.
He lands awry and bumps a tree,
"Oh, not again!" laughs nearby Louie.

A family of ducks, in formation neat,
Decides it's time for a splashy treat.
They leap and flap, but who's the boss?
In icy waters, no such gloss!

An old man with a frown so tight,
Walks on ice, but slips with fright.
He spins around, catches a glance,
And laughs, "Guess I'm part of this dance!"

At sunset, the ice glows anymore,
Reflecting all, it's quite the score.
With giggles echoing through the chill,
Winter's humor does fit the bill!

Light Beneath the Ice

A penguin slips with style and grace,
He takes a dive, what a funny face!
The fish below give him a cheer,
As he surfaces, his smile quite clear.

They float like dreams on a glassy sheet,
Wobbling still, they have happy feet.
The snowflakes giggle as they fall,
The laughter echoes, a winter's call.

A hare pops up with a curious glance,
He spots the penguin in a funny dance.
They share a laugh in the chilly breeze,
Turning cold into warmth with playful tease.

As night creeps in, the stars twinkle bright,
Wishing for silliness under soft moonlight.
Every frosty face wears a grin wide,
On this icy stage, joy won't slide!

The Peaceful Expanse

A moose stands still, looking quite daft,
With ice beneath, he's a comedic craft.
He tries to skate but stumbles instead,
His awkward moves make the laughter spread.

A squirrel zooms by on a wooden sled,
Making snowballs, while feeling well-fed.
He plops one down right on a chap,
Who yells 'Oh no!' as he takes a nap.

The trees lean in, they can hardly breathe,
For nature's laughter, it's hard to leave.
As snowmen chuckle with carrot eyes,
Their warmth of spirit truly belies.

Amidst the stillness, fun times arise,
In whispered winds where the humor lies.
The ice may be cold, but hearts are warm,
Playing in winter is the perfect charm!

Slumbering Skies

Clouds float gently, a sleepy sigh,
With dreams that dance, oh me, oh my!
A bear snores softly, wrapped in white fluff,
Chasing sweet dreams of berry-filled stuff.

A fox tiptoes by, with a twinkle in eyes,
Sneaking a peek at the bear's cozy lie.
With a playful nudge, he makes a quick dash,
The bear grumbles softly, but oh, what a clash!

Stars sprinkle humor, like glistening dust,
In night's embrace, there's laughter and trust.
Beneath the still sky, mischief unfolds,
As nature's tale of fun is retold.

The moon winks down on this frosty show,
While dreams play tag in the glimmering glow.
In slumbering skies, joy takes a flight,
Leaving cold behind, as warmth feels just right!

Beneath the Feathered White

A duck quacks loudly, 'Follow my lead!'
With flapping wings, she plants a good deed.
She opens a path through the soft, deep snow,
While mischief brews like a warming glow.

A snowball fight breaks as kids begin,
Laughter erupts, oh where to begin?
Rolling white hills become forts and shields,
Masterpieces form in the snowy fields.

An owl hoots softly, a chuckle escapes,
Watching the antics of all the young shapes.
With each playful throw, a burst of delight,
The spirit of fun shines oh-so-bright!

Beneath the feathers, the warmth starts to grow,
In crisp, cold air, joy's warmth gets to flow.
With giggles and grins, the wintry fun calls,
As laughter melts down these frosty walls.

A Silent Palette of White

A blanket of white, what a sight,
The ducks think it's snow, oh what a fright!
They waddle around, with a quack and a cheer,
Fashion faux pas, every day of the year.

Laughter erupts as the ice starts to crack,
The penguins slide by with a silly knack.
They dance on the ice, a slip-and-slide craze,
Who knew that cold could bring such warm praise?

Snowmen conferring on top of the hill,
Debating the best way to give folks a thrill.
With carrots for noses, they stand so bold,
While we all wonder who'll melt first in the cold.

So come tiptoe lightly, enjoy the bizarre,
The frigid pranksters are never too far.
With laughter and joy, let the fun abound,
In this frosty paradise, silliness found!

Hushed Notes of Winter

Whispers of snowflakes, they gently descend,
While polar bears chuckle with each little bend.
They play tag on the ice, with grins wide and merry,
The only catch: don't let the seals know you're hairy!

A snowball fight ensues, who will take the crown?
The seals pull a heist, and they steal the renown.
With flippers a-flap, they roll with delight,
The laughter of winter is quite a strange sight.

In igloos adorned with the finest of furs,
The comedians twirl with their best winter purrs.
The rabbits all giggle, concealing their noses,
While they play hide and seek among frosty roses.

When the night settles in, the moon starts to glow,
Each critter's a superstar, putting on quite the show.
With snowflakes as confetti, the laughter will soar,
In this winter wonderland, who could ask for more?

Echoes in the Frosted Void

An echo of laughter from the trees up high,
As squirrels in pajamas are passing by.
They boast of their stash of acorns so grand,
While slipping and sliding on their frosty land!

Frogs in wool sweaters, croaking a tune,
Jumping and jiving 'neath the bright winter moon.
From snowdrifts they leap with ridiculous flair,
While the owls hoot advice, "Just don't lose your hair!"

The foxes roll in snow, oh what a sight,
With mischief aplenty, they plot through the night.
New disguises, they craft from the snow and the ice,
Maybe they'll fool the geese once or twice!

With giggles and joy, this frosty retreat,
Push sleds down the hill or just chatter and eat.
In dreams wrapped in white, where the laughter is bold,
Every snowy moment's a treasure to hold!

When the World Holds Its Breath

The world holds its breath in a whimsical state,
While snowflakes engage in a frosty debate.
Are we really just magic? Or puddles in spring?
The debate gets quite heated, oh what can we bring?

A sleigh ride erupts, with hot cocoa spills,
The joy of the season ignites all our thrills.
With sleds packed with chuckles and grins ear to ear,
Wintertime shenanigans—now let's all cheer!

The trees wear their white like a silly ol' hat,
As squirrels frolic by, chattering chat.
A snowman is dancing, so we join the spree,
But let's keep it quiet, or we'll wake up the sea!

At dusk, with the stars twinkling bright overhead,
We whisper our secrets, "Will the ice ever spread?"
In this merriment brief, where the world takes a pause,
We find joy in the hush, and we laugh without cause!

The Depth of Silence

In the hush of the cold, they all took a nap,
A squirrel on skis had a slippery flap.
The fish wore tuxedos, looking quite neat,
While snowflakes giggled, dancing to the beat.

A penguin slid by, with a wink and a grin,
Challenged a bear to a secretive spin.
The ice laughed aloud, cracking jokes from below,
And snowmen chattered about the best show.

All the trees were dressed in crystalline coats,
Swapping tall tales, and plotting to boast.
A rabbit made snowballs, with a flick of his foot,
While the geese played cards, oh what a hoot!

As the sun peeked through, hearts began to warm,
The ice held its breath, in a magical charm.
With laughter unheard, in the sly winter light,
They frolicked and played in this frozen delight.

In the Heart of the Freeze

Inside a chill box, where antics unfold,
Bears wear pajamas, if truth be told.
With frost-covered dreams, they contemplate cheer,
While ants throw a party, bringing snacks that are dear.

A moose mixes cocoa, quite clumsy at best,
And the owls play Monopoly, never at rest.
The beavers are builders, but slacking today,
Deciding instead to just lounge and play.

When icicles shimmer in the bright midday sun,
The lizards start tangoing, having so much fun.
The snowballs were flying, no one was still,
Even the wind joined in, giving a thrill.

In the heart of the freeze, mirth knows no bounds,
Where the foolish meet frosty, and laughter resounds.
With giggles transpiring and craziness rife,
In the chill of the scene, they found warmth in life.

Slumbering Reflections

Under a blanket of icy white fluff,
The world was asleep, but not all was tough.
A fox dreamed of sushi, we chuckled so hard,
While a bear in a beanie played guard with a card.

The fish had a union, demanding a feast,
While snowmen molded some hot springs at least.
A mirror of laughter, in frosted repose,
Balloons floated by with a party of crows.

While the icicles twinkled and winked in the night,
The animals gathered — what a delightful sight!
Sing songs of the snow, let the merriment flow,
Through the wintery hush, with a warm, joyful glow.

As the stars twinkled down, the dreams took to flight,
In slumbering reflections, a whimsical night.
And when morning came, those wanderers leapt,
In the spirit of play, the zoo never slept.

Dances with Frost

Once a time there were critters with ice-skating grace,
They twirled and they whirled, in this frosty place.
A walrus in tutu was leading the way,
While a rabbit in skates joined this playful ballet.

A tap-dancing penguin made everyone smile,
And the otters built trains to show off their style.
With giggles and grins, they formed quite a crew,
The frosty ones danced, 'til the daylight broke through.

The trees all reclined, swaying heads to the beat,
With icicles chiming, oh what a feat!
They marveled at jokes that snowflakes would wield,
In this magical moment, their hearts could not yield.

With laughter still ringing, and winter on song,
The dances with frost, where all creatures belong.
And as night draped the world, like a quilt oh so grand,
They tucked in for the sleep, hand in paw, paw in hand.

Fables of the Frosty Dream

In a world where penguins dance,
And polar bears wear knit cap pants,
The snowmen have a wild debate,
On which one's carrot nose looks great.

A sledding cat with fancy flair,
Glides down hills without a care,
While frostbit toes are quite a sight,
They laugh and sing with pure delight.

I heard a tale of a moose named Lou,
Who fancied himself a ballet shoe,
He leapt and twirled on icy ground,
While all the critters gathered 'round.

As whispers floated on the breeze,
Of snowy capers and wild make-believes,
They chuckled loud in winter's sun,
In a frosty land, where fun's never done.

Wandering Through Shimmering Night

Beneath the moon, a llama pranced,
In snowflake shoes, it got entranced,
With twirls and spins, it made a show,
As owls hooted, "Bravo! Bravo!"

A rabbit tried to build a den,
But ended up with snowball men,
They donned top hats and gave a bow,
While giggling softly, oh, wow, wow!

The stars above began to wink,
While chilly winds asked if they think,
That penguins can play chess at night,
With ice cubes clinking in delight.

The ice cat sang a lullaby,
As turtles wore their coats awry,
In this shimmering, silly scene,
Where winter dreams are light and keen.

Reflections in the Quiet Abyss

A fish in shades of purple hue,
Thought it could learn to ski, who knew?
It zipped and flipped, oh, what a sight,
Until it landed, right on its light!

A snowflake fell and got a fright,
When it saw a squirrel in mid-flight,
It twirled around in pure surprise,
As acorns scattered from the skies.

There's chatter from a crafty fox,
Who's building castles from cardboard blocks,
With penguins serving icy tea,
In this whimsical jamboree.

When winter's breath plays tricks and fun,
And creatures frolic, one by one,
They spin, they laugh, a joyous buzz,
In the abyss, that's what it does!

When Night and Snow Converge

At twilight's glow, a beaver sighed,
With dreams of winning snowball pride,
While shoveling snow with great finesse,
Claiming, "I'm a snowball champ, no less!"

A hedgehog rolled, creating lines,
And wrote sweet poems about the pines,
With words that danced on icy air,
Bringing giggles everywhere!

The wise old owl sat up so high,
Watching creatures laugh and fly,
As snowflakes tickled each small nose,
In this fun-fueled night that glows.

So let us all embrace the night,
With silly dreams and sheer delight,
For in this world where laughter blends,
We find true joy that never ends.

Chilling Silence at Dusk

In the still of the night so clear,
A snowman sneezed, oh dear, oh dear!
He lost his hat, it flew away,
And now he's feeling quite dismay.

The moon laughs in the frosty air,
While turtles skedaddle, unaware.
Penguins waddle, slipping with grace,
Wishing for a warmer place!

Icicles hang like frozen tears,
As squirrels plot shenanigans near.
They throw snowballs, chuckle with glee,
Making snow angels—oh, whoopee!

In this hush, a laughter flows,
Beneath the stars, anything goes.
When the sun wakes, with its glow,
We'll laugh at the fun from below!

Dreams Beneath the Glaze

Bubbles form in a frosty stream,
A moose gets stuck—oh, how absurd it seems!
With ice skates on, he twirls in style,
While birds giggle, they can't help but smile.

A bear in a scarf, so finely knit,
Tries to dance but falls with a split.
The otters chuckle and slide on by,
Making wave noises, oh my, oh my!

With dreams under shimmering cover,
The snowflakes sprinkle, we all discover,
That winter's charm isn't quite a bore,
When you trip on snow and laugh some more!

In every sparkle, a joke is told,
In every breath, the cold grows bold.
So gather 'round and join the cheer,
For winter silliness is finally here!

Frosted Canvas of Night

Upon the white, the stars take flight,
Where paper cranes dance in delight.
A fox in pajamas, how silly it seems,
Invites the night to share in dreams.

He prances and twirls, kicks up some snow,
With a grin, he shouts, "Look at me go!"
The snowflakes respond with a gentle tease,
As the night air fills with a playful breeze.

Rabbits in toques hop with flair,
Planning a snowball fight, oh what a scare!
They dodge and weave, plotting with zest,
Each bounce a giggle, they're truly the best.

Under soft light of a lantern's beam,
We relish in laughter, frozen in dream.
With this frosted canvas, we all gleam bright,
Creating our stories under the night!

Murmurs of the Silent Waters

In the whisper of the chilled night air,
A cat tries skating; oh, what a scare!
She slips and tumbles, right on her back,
While the fish below plan a prank attack.

The geese gossip, huddled in a row,
"Did you see her slide? She's putting on a show!"
With flippers out, they mimic her fall,
Creating a joy that enchants us all.

Upon the rim, the frost peeks and pranks,
As sheep march in, giving night their thanks.
They line up and pose, a comical sight,
Counting their giggles, which equal delight.

The waters chuckle and ripple with cheer,
As the tales of the night bubble near.
Each murmur a secret, a funny little tease,
In this world of wonder, we do as we please!

An Overture of Frozen Whispers

On the ice I see a grin,
A penguin sliding with a spin.
He wears a hat that's far too big,
And tries to dance a silly jig.

Nearby a seal with squeaky shoes,
Takes a leap and sings the blues.
He floats around like it's a game,
While all the fish just chant his name.

Snowflakes fall like confetti bright,
They twirl and swirl in the crisp night.
A fox in boots attempts a flip,
And lands right on a fishy slip.

With laughter echoing 'cross the plain,
The critters join in a joyous refrain.
Who knew the chill could bring such cheer?
In this chilly world, we lose our fear.

Still Waters Reflecting Stars

Beneath the glow of twinkling light,
A moose wears skates, ready for flight.
He slips and slides with hopeful glee,
A ballerina, but not quite free.

The stars above just crack a smile,
As ice fish swim in playful style.
A pike dressed up in a tiny bow,
Says, "Look at me, I'm stealing the show!"

The otters race in a slippery dash,
Their giggles echo with every splash.
A family of ducks waddle in line,
Singing sweet quacks, oh so divine.

With each twirl and playful cheer,
The winter night is full of cheer.
These moments bring such joyful jest,
In nature's realm, we feel so blessed.

Tranquility in the Chill

In the stillness, a snowman sighs,
He's got a carrot nose, but no good thighs.
He dreams of summer, sun, and sand,
But for now, he's in a frosty band.

A rabbit hops, and slips so fast,
Break dancing while the cold winds blast.
With a puffy coat and mismatched socks,
He's the life of the party, full of knocks!

The ice cracks softly underfoot,
As a bear in shades starts to strut.
"Check me out, I'm too cool to freeze!"
While squirrels giggle from the trees.

We revel in these frozen scenes,
In a world of laughter, love, and dreams.
Each chilly chuckle, a story spun,
In this realm, we're always fun!

Glistening Dreams on Ice

Underneath a sky so bright,
A lazy cat dreams in pure delight.
His paws are cold, his heart so warm,
While snowflakes gather, a perfect swarm.

A turtle on skates takes a slow ride,
With a wind-up toy that's full of pride.
He scoots past a bush that cold winds swish,
Then says, "I'm just here to make a wish!"

Wonders dance upon the rim,
As ice bears play a jazzy whim.
They wiggle and jiggle, oh what a sight,
Making the most of this frosty night.

In this land of chilly jest,
Every creature knows they're blessed.
With laughter echoing through the trees,
In this world, we do as we please.

The Hushed Cradle of Snow

A snowman sits, wearing my hat,
Daring the sun, 'Come, let's chat!'
His carrot nose, a comical sight,
Wishing on clouds that float so light.

Sleds zoom by with squeals of glee,
Who knew winter could bring such spree?
In yards, we build castles with flair,
King and queen? Just a snowflake in hair.

Tongue stuck on a frosty pole,
Laughter erupts - we've reached our goal!
Snowball fights start without a care,
The snow is soft, but beware the glare!

With winter's breath as our blanket tight,
We snuggle close, through the chilly night.
In this quiet bliss, we find our fun,
Chasing snowflakes, 'til the day is done.

Frosted Serenity

Flakes fall down like tiny fluff,
We gather 'round, it's never enough!
A snowman contest - who's the best?
Judges are crows, they won't let us rest!

Sipping cocoa, oh so hot,
What's that? My marshmallow just shot!
It soared like a flying dream,
Right into Dad's whipped cream stream.

Frosty breath and giggles loud,
We dance like we're on a cloud.
The ice cracks, oops! We nearly slide,
But laughing together, we take it in stride.

This winter wonderland's quite deranged,
Yet here we are, simply unchanged.
With frosty shenanigans in the mix,
We're living our silly winter fix.

Enchanted by the Winter's Lullaby

Night falls softly on cotton white,
Snowmen wave to the moon in delight.
Yet here I sit, cake on my lap,
Dreaming of journeys, not a mishap.

Icicles dangle from rooftops like jewels,
Tripping my brother, oh, he fools!
"Catch me if you can" I burst and flee,
But land on my face, oh what a spree!

Snow angels crafted in giggles and snow,
Each one claiming, 'Look how I glow!'
But really it's just a frosty paste,
Who knew joy could be so misplaced?

In this winter's warmth, we find our cheer,
With muffled laughter and shouts we hear.
Beneath this blanket of cold, right in the center,
Life's unpredictable, but oh, what a splendor!

Unspoken Visions in the Cold

Chilling winds play a tune so sweet,
In frozen parks, we shuffle our feet.
A surprise falling snowball hits me right,
Just wanted peace, but now it's fight!

Pikes on skates twirl with grace,
Until someone lands on the wrong place.
Faceplanting in glimmering white,
Creating memories in the frosty night.

Sipping hot tea, we whisper dreams,
I swear I saw a bigfoot it seems.
He waved and danced, oh what a tale,
Or was it another snowman frail?

Under stars that dazzle on this bright night,
We share our secrets, hearts feeling light.
In laughter and warmth, the cold disappears,
Creating new dreams, amidst all our cheers.